Grasping
the fading light

A Journey through PTSD

Julie Bloss Kelsey

Cover art by Anania Kocharyan, *Wind* 2020

Author photo credit to Neisha Williams

Book cover and design by Sadie Butterworth-Jones
www.luneviewpublishing.co.uk

ISBN 978-0-936481-24-1

Jacar Press
6617 Deerview Trail
Durham, NC 27712
www.jacarpress.com

Sable Books
www.sablebooks.org

P retending
T hat childhood
S exual assault
D oesn't still haunt me

sliver of moon
still hanging on
to my illusions

grasping the fading light
bare talons
of an old oak

cold hands
grip my shoulders –
the brittle wings
of a pinned
butterfly

river birch —
peeling back memories
of spring

flaking paint
on the siding of my house
how can I look away
from these unflattering pieces
of my life

homemade frosting –
attempting to cover cracks
in the façade

first morning coffee lies I tell myself

nor'easter
an unexpected bite
in my apple

a gap
in my memory —
discarded
on the closet floor
in fetal position

my heart
a hollowed-out pumpkin
mid-November rain

autumn sky —
the stars have drifted
far from home...
beneath my eyes
deep shadows

shaking sand dollars
to hear angel wings inside
as a child
I never questioned
the ways I was broken

free will to do what you say bully pulpit

December chill
your false smile
breezing by
my temper rising
with the moon

chess board
I knock you off
your pedestal

stripping away the patriarchy naked Barbies

winter wind —
the raptor's wings
waver

damned if I do
damned if I don't
trauma therapy

if I let go
the whole world
will fall to pieces...
shattered
snow globe

crystal wind —
a thousand icy stars
in my eyes

winter sky
the sun just a faint
yellow smudge —
unable to complete anything
on my to-do list

reciting
the alphabet...
all of the ways
I have failed
myself

driving past
the trauma unit
wishing
I could drop off
my inner child

every week the same
tangled branches outside
my therapist's window

scraping away
layer upon layer
of brokenness
underneath lies
a child's room

in the waiting room
I search for any sign
of my recovery...
such bright stripes
on this clownfish

reminding myself
crazy isn't contagious
doesn't help...
I rush home
to take a shower

mockingbird —
so many things
I wish I could say

snowmelt —
things I thought
I'd left behind

recovered memories
no one believes —
my failed efforts
to piece myself
back together

low-lying clouds —
suppressing
the urge to cry

granite thunderhead —
my whole life
insignificant

frayed rope
the last of my emotions
betrays me

the black mark
on my permanent record —
molestation

blackout drunk —
I come to my senses
during karaoke

IN SOMe NIghtmare Again

my inner children
violated one by one...
dominoes

self-mutilation —
the scars you see
the scars you don't

fireworks...
pop pop popping
painkillers

medicated —
the haze between
sea and sky

crepuscular rays —
I book another appointment
for therapy

thermals rising
all across the valley
prayers for rain

in a holding pattern
above the Chesapeake
...virga

a knot of sparrows
rearranges itself
on the power line...
I wait for my story
to unravel

watching the geese fly
in and out of formation —
evening sky

in a broken mirror
fragments of my younger selves
...this fractal timeline

remembering
what it was like
before I knew

summer drizzle
lingering on my porch
a blue damselfly

the sketchbook
I keep in the back
of my closet —
so much of my life
left untouched

three shoeboxes of letters:
I attempt to pack up
childhood

webbed moon
my elusive search
for closure

after the lightning strike
a thunderclap
headache

if I can't even
control my own body
how can I hope
to change the world...
chronic illness

one step forward
two steps back
three-day migraine

beneath the pounding
of a construction site
the creek's burble

holding myself
to a higher standard
I need to stop
apologizing
for my own existence

cloudbreak —
my inner child
takes my hand

barrier island —
the bray of wild horses
drifts on sea breeze

through wooden slats
of a horse paddock
the child's eye

flashbacks —
my lost pieces
finally come home

the missing windows
in my sand castle —
sea glass

reunified
I find myself
at the beach —
driftwood arms full
of seaweed blankets

cirrus at sunset —
a line of fire rainbows
ignite the ocean

Epilogue

I hope
my next life is wild
and untamed
...shameless

Publication Credits

My thanks to the editors of these fine publications in which these poems first appeared, some in slightly different form:

A Hundred Gourds

Bright Stars, An Organic Tanka Anthology, Volume 1, January 2014

Dance into the World, Tanka Society of America Members' Anthology, 2020

Diogen

Englyn: Journal of Four Line Poetry

ephemerae

Failed Haiku

#FemkuMag

Frameless Sky

Fresh Out

hedgerow: a journal of small poems

Human/Kind

Lifting the Sky: Southwestern Haiku & Haiga,
Dos Gatos Press, 2013

lisnin 2 jazz, Towpath Anthology 2020

Moonbathing

moongarlic E-zine

Paper Mountains: 2020 Seabeck Haiku Getaway Anthology

Prune Juice Journal

Ribbons

Scryptic

Sharpening the Green Pencil, The Book of the Contest 2015

Stacking Stones, An Anthology of Short Tanka Sequences

The Math Haiku Project, September 4, 2020

Award Credits

(some poems appeared in slightly different forms)

"a knot of sparrows," Honorable Mention,
Mandy's Pages Annual Tanka Contest, August 2018

"barrier island," Honorable Mention,
2017 Betty Drevniok Awards, May 2017

"every week the same," Second Place,
23rd International "Kusamakura" Haiku Competition,
November 2018

"free will," Honorable Mention, Marlene Mountain
Memorial Haiku Contest, 2021

"snowmelt," Shortlisted, Second Annual H. Gene Murtha
Memorial Senryu Contest, July 2017

"stripping away," Winner, Marlene Mountain
Memorial Haiku Contest, July 2018

Acknowledgements

I would like to thank Kala Ramesh, judge of the 2021 Sable Books Haiku Contest for Women, for reading my poetry with a compassionate heart. My appreciation also goes to Autumn Noelle Hall and Kate MacQueen, the primary readers for this contest. Thanks for giving my manuscript a chance. My gratitude extends to Natalie Eleanor Patterson, Richard Krawiec, and everyone at Sable Books for providing me the opportunity to share my journey with others. I'd also like to acknowledge Rowan Beckett — my earliest pieces about trauma were published in their groundbreaking journals. Rowan Beckett, thanks for giving my work a home.

Many people have held space for me during this journey of healing, my poetic trek across the pages of this collection, or both, including John Kelsey, Robert and Carol Bloss, Sara and Neisha Williams, Christina DiEdoardo, Susan Burch, Laura Olesen-Berge, Tia Haynes, Jennifer Rueckemann, Debbie Byrd,

Carol Lloyd, Nicki Wells, Robin Anna Smith, Ilene Krom, Erin Raedeke, Heather Jauquet, Dolores Green, Monica Parham, Lisa Domagala, Sandra Stalzer, Bryan Rickert, and my kids Mark, Mikey & Jay. Thank you for everything. My love to you all.

A round of hugs also goes to the therapists who helped me, and all of my support groups, past and present. You mean the world to me.

About the Author

Julie Bloss Kelsey's award-winning short-form poetry has appeared in publications spanning the globe, including the United States, Canada, Croatia, England, India, and Japan. She won the 2022 Jane Reichhold Haiga Contest in the Photographic/Mixed Media category, and was named the DC Area Winner for the Golden Haiku Poetry Contest in 2021. Her first chapbook of poetry, *The Call of Wildflowers*, is available for free online through Moth Orchid Press (formerly Title IX Press). She is currently on the board of The Haiku Foundation, where she pens a column entitled *New to Haiku*. Julie lives in suburban Maryland with her husband and kids.

Made in the USA
Middletown, DE
18 June 2023

32330416R00029